MathFlare

Name: _____

Class: _____

Teacher: _____

Introduction

As parents and educators, we recognize the pivotal role mathematics plays in shaping a child's academic journey and future success. Yet, the path to mathematical proficiency can often seem daunting, fraught with challenges and complexities. That's where the transformative power of MathFlare Workbooks shine through, illuminating the way forward with clarity, precision, and purpose.

Introducing MathFlare Workbooks – a beacon of guidance, a testament to excellence, and a catalyst for achievement. Crafted with meticulous care and expertise, MathFlare Workbooks stand as paragons of educational excellence, designed to nurture young minds, ignite a passion for learning, and develop a deep-rooted understanding of mathematical concepts.

Picture this: your child eagerly delves into the pages of Mathflare Workbook, greeted by a step-by-step guide illuminated with vivid examples that demystify complex mathematical concepts. With each turn of the page, they embark on a journey of discovery, encountering thoughtfully curated practice questions that reinforce learning and hone problem-solving skills. And when they unveil the answers to those very questions, a sense of accomplishment blossoms within them – a tangible reward for their hard work and dedication.

But MathFlare Workbooks are more than just tools for learning; they are pathways to comprehension, fostering a deep-seated understanding of mathematical concepts through a sequential, logical flow. From fundamental principles to advanced problem-solving strategies, every chapter builds upon the last, ensuring a robust foundation upon which future knowledge can be constructed.

As parents, we yearn for nothing more than to see our children thrive, to witness the spark of inspiration ignited within them as they conquer academic challenges with confidence and poise. MathFlare Workbooks serve as partners in this noble endeavor, offering not just practice questions, but the keys to unlocking a world of opportunity.

And for teachers, MathFlare Workbooks stand as invaluable allies in the quest to cultivate mathematical proficiency in the classroom. With answers readily available, instructors can focus on guiding and nurturing their students, confident in the knowledge that MathFlare Workbooks provide a solid framework upon which to build.

In the pages of MathFlare Workbooks, we find not just the promise of academic excellence, but the seeds of a brighter tomorrow. So let us embrace the power of mathematics, let us champion the journey of learning, and let us pave the way for a generation of young minds poised to shape the world. With MathFlare Workbooks as our guide, the possibilities are infinite, and the future, bright.

Table of Contents

MathFlare — MATH WORKBOOK — Grade 2
Step by Step Guide and Essential Practice with Answers
- Addition Subtraction
- Multiplication
- Place Value and Expanded Notations
- Geometry

MathFlare — MATH WORKBOOK — Grade 2-3
Step by Step Guide and Essential Practice with Answers
- Addition Subtraction
- Multiplication and Division
- Place Value and Expanded Notations
- Geometry

MathFlare — MATH WORKBOOK — Grade 3
Step by Step Guide and Essential Practice with Answers
- Multiplication and Division
- Decimals
- Place Value and Expanded Notations
- Fractions and Geometry

MathFlare — MATH WORKBOOK — Grade 1
Step by Step Guide and Essential Practice with Answers
- Counting and Numbers
- Addition and Subtraction
- Place Value and Expanded Notations
- Understanding Time

MathFlare — MATH WORKBOOK — Grade 1-2
Step by Step Guide and Essential Practice with Answers
- Counting and Numbers
- Addition and Subtraction
- Place Value and Expanded Notations
- Understanding Time

MathFlare — MATH WORKBOOK — Grade 3-4
Step by Step Guide and Essential Practice with Answers
- Addition Subtraction
- Multiplication Division
- Place Value and Expanded Notations
- Fractions and Geometry

MathFlare — MATH WORKBOOK — Grade 4
Step by Step Guide and Essential Practice with Answers
- Addition Subtraction
- Multiplication Division
- Place Value and Expanded Notations
- Fractions and Geometry

MathFlare — MATH WORKBOOK — Grade 4-5
Step by Step Guide and Essential Practice with Answers
- Multiplication Division
- Place Value and Expanded Notations
- Fractions and Geometry
- Unit Conversion

MathFlare MATH WORKBOOK

Grade 5
Step by Step Guide and Essential Practice with Answers
- Multiplication Division
- Place Value and Expanded Notations
- Fractions and Geometry
- Unit Conversion

MathFlare Publishing

Grade 5-6
Step by Step Guide and Essential Practice with Answers
- Multiplication Division
- Place Value and Expanded Notations
- Fractions and Geometry
- Units and Statistics

MathFlare Publishing

Grade 6
Step by Step Guide and Essential Practice with Answers
- Integers and Statistics
- Arithmetic and Pre-Algebra
- Fractions and Geometry
- Ratio and Percentage

MathFlare Publishing

Grade 6-7
Step by Step Guide and Essential Practice with Answers
- Arithmetic and Pre-Algebra
- Ratio, Percent Proportion
- Geometry
- Statistics

MathFlare Publishing

Grade 7
Step by Step Guide and Essential Practice with Answers
- Pre-Algebra
- Ratio, Percent Proportion
- Geometry
- Statistics

MathFlare Publishing

Grade 7-8
Step by Step Guide and Essential Practice with Answers
- Pre-Algebra
- Ratio, Percent Proportion
- Geometry and Cartesian Plane
- Statistics

MathFlare Publishing

Grade 8-9
Step by Step Guide and Essential Practice with Answers
- Pre-Algebra
- Ratio, Proportion and Percentage
- Linear Equations
- Geometry and Cartesian Plane

MathFlare Publishing

Grade 8
Step by Step Guide and Essential Practice with Answers
- Pre-Algebra
- Percentage
- Linear Equations
- Geometry

MathFlare Publishing

Place Value and Expanded Notations

Place value tells us the value of a digit in a number based on where it's placed.

Imagine we have the number 5,987,647.52843. It has 12 digits.

Now, each digit holds a special place. Let's break down the number 5,987,647.52843:

- The digit 5 is in the millions place. Its value is 5 × 1,000,000=5,000,000.

- The digit 9 is in the hundred thousands place. Its value is 9×100,000=900,000.

- The digit 8 is in the ten thousands place. Its value is 8×10,000=80,000.

- The digit 7 is in the thousands place. Its value is 7×1,000=7,000.

- The digit 6 is in the hundreds place. Its value is 6×100=600.

- The digit 4 is in the tens place. Its value is 4×10=40.

- The digit 7 is in the ones place. Its value is 7×1=7.

- The digit 5 is in the tenths place. Its value is $5 \times \frac{1}{10} = 0.5$.

- The digit 2 is in the hundredths place. Its value is $2 \times \frac{1}{100} = 0.02$.

- The digit 8 is in the thousandths place. Its value is $8 \times \frac{1}{1000} = 0.008$.

- The digit 4 is in the ten thousandths place. Its value is $4 \times \frac{1}{10,000} = 0.0004$.

- The digit 3 is in the hundred thousandths place. Its value is $3 \times \dfrac{1}{100,000} =$ 0.00003.

When we add these values together, we find the value of the entire number:

$$5,000,000 + 900,000 + 80,000 + 7,000 + 600 + 40 + 7 + 0.5 + 0.02 + 0.008$$
$$+0.0004 + 0.00003 = 5,987,647.52843$$

Let's solve some problems:

Place value of the underlined digit:

9,216.46795 = **5 hundred thousandths**

Expanded notations:

442,218.932   4 hundred thousands + 4 ten thousands + 2 thousands + 2 hundreds + 1 ten + 8 ones + 9 tenths + 3 hundredths + 2 thousandths

81,315,897.3   80,000,000 + 1,000,000 + 300,000 + 10,000 + 5,000 + 800 + 90 + 7 + 0.3

50,131,193.9   5 ten millions + 1 hundred thousand + 3 ten thousands + 1 thousand + 1 hundred + 9 tens + 3 ones + 9 tenths

Rounding Numbers

Rounding numbers is the process of approximating a numerical value to a certain degree of accuracy by replacing it with a simpler or more convenient value. Rounding is commonly used to simplify calculations and express numbers in a more manageable form.

Steps to Rounding Numbers:

1. **Identify the digit to be rounded:** Determine the digit to which the number will be rounded.

2. **Look at the next digit:** Examine the digit immediately to the right of the one being rounded.

3. **Decide whether to round up or down:** If the next digit is 5 or greater, round the digit up. If it is less than 5, round the digit down.

4. **Adjust the number:** Change the digit being rounded and replace all digits to the right with zeros if necessary.

Properties of Rounding Numbers:

1. **Accuracy:** Rounding reduces the precision of a number but maintains its approximate value.

2. **Simplicity:** Rounding simplifies calculations by using fewer digits.

3. **Ease of Use:** Rounding makes numbers easier to work with, especially in mental arithmetic and estimation.

Methods of Rounding Numbers:

1. **Round to Nearest Integer:** Round to the nearest whole number.

    I.   Round Up (Ceiling): Always round up to the nearest integer.

    II.   Round Down (Floor): Always round down to the nearest integer.

2. **Round to Nearest Tenth:** Round to the nearest tenth (one decimal place).

3. **Round to Nearest Hundredth:** Round to the nearest hundredth (two decimal places).

4. **Round to Nearest Thousandth:** Round to the nearest thousandth (three decimal places).

5. **Round to Specific Decimal Places:** Round to a specified number of decimal places as needed.

Let's round the number **438,576.214** to various degrees of accuracy:

Rounding Level	Rounded Number	Difference from Original
Nearest Whole Number	438,576	0
Nearest Ten	438,580	+4
Nearest Hundred	438,600	+24
Nearest Thousand	439,000	+424
Nearest Ten Thousand	440,000	+3,424
Nearest Hundred Thousand	400,000	−38,576
Nearest Million	0.4386×10^6	−438,576.214

Place Value

Determine the place value of the underlined digit.

1. 8,727,381.6<u>1</u> = _____

2. <u>2</u>,941,502.35 = _____

3. 1,<u>0</u>34,919.75 = _____

4. 3,6<u>1</u>8,964.38 = _____

5. 9,220,2<u>6</u>2.9 = _____

6. <u>4</u>,348,690.72 = _____

7. 5,898,18<u>6</u>.26 = _____

8. 9,728,5̲15.15 = _____

9. 7,665,94̲7.38 = _____

10. 2,72̲4,441.7 = _____

11. 2,087,120.5̲1 = _____

12. 1,075,8̲95.09 = _____

13. 1,87̲1,450.23 = _____

14. 3,016,991̲.32 = _____

15. 6,714,566.6̲2 = _____

16. 3,5<u>6</u>5,102.83 = _____

17. 2,258,139.4<u>4</u> = _____

18. <u>2</u>,561,938.88 = _____

19. 1,951,<u>4</u>41.82 = _____

20. 7,905,<u>6</u>36.54 = _____

21. 7,677,2<u>3</u>1.72 = _____

22. 3,81<u>0</u>,604.1 = _____

23. 7,572,<u>7</u>95.39 = _____

24. 2,741,<u>0</u>18.95 = _____

25. 8,518,526.2<u>7</u> = _____

26. 6,642,<u>5</u>48.91 = _____

27. <u>6</u>,738,105.14 = _____

28. <u>6</u>,579,480.26 = _____

29. 7,16<u>4</u>,456.96 = _____

30. 8,161,951.<u>2</u>5 = _____

31. 2,654,<u>3</u>84.95 = _____

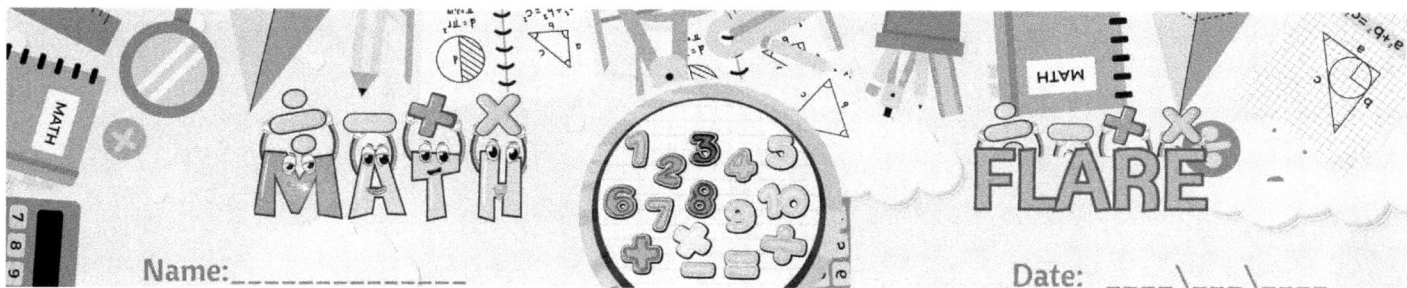

Name:_____ Date: _____

32. 6,040,362.7 = _____

33. 5,108,112.79 = _____

34. 5,165,399.57 = _____

35. 7,982,633.97 = _____

36. 1,734,874.42 = _____

37. 5,087,522.68 = _____

38. 6,044,192.55 = _____

39. 2,945,636.73 = _____

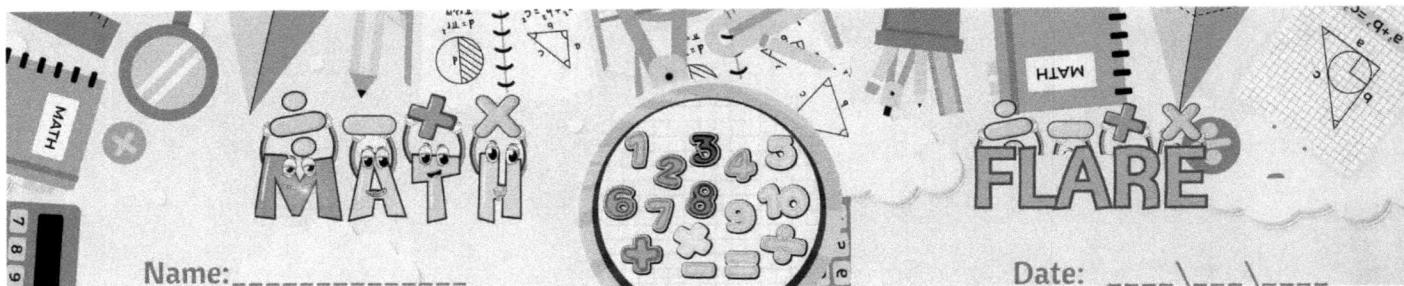

Place Value: Expanded Notation

Provide the expanded notation for each value.

40. _____   3 ten thousands + 2 thousands + 5 hundreds + 9 tens + 6 ones + 6 tenths + 5 hundredths

41. _____   1 ten thousand + 7 thousands + 6 hundreds + 8 tens + 1 one + 7 tenths + 8 hundredths

42. _____   9 ten thousands + 8 hundreds + 9 tens + 2 ones + 4 tenths + 6 hundredths

43. _____   3 ten thousands + 8 thousands + 7 hundreds + 6 ones + 3 tenths + 2 hundredths

44. _____   7 ten thousands + 1 thousand + 2 hundreds + 8 tens + 5 tenths

45. _____   3 ten thousands + 4 thousands + 8 tens + 3 ones + 7 tenths + 1 hundredth

46. _____   5 ten thousands + 5 thousands + 7 tens + 9 tenths + 3 hundredths

47. _____   1 ten thousand + 8 thousands + 1 hundred + 4 tens + 4 ones + 5 tenths + 6 hundredths

48. _____   7 ten thousands + 8 hundreds + 2 tens + 9 ones + 7 hundredths

49. _____   9 ten thousands + 4 thousands + 4 hundreds + 8 tens + 5 ones + 7 tenths + 7 hundredths

50. _____   7 ten thousands + 5 thousands + 9 hundreds + 7 tens + 6 ones + 9 tenths + 4 hundredths

51. _____   5 ten thousands + 8 thousands + 2 hundreds + 1 ten + 3 ones + 8 hundredths

52. _____   5 ten thousands + 2 thousands + 7 hundreds + 2 tens + 1 one + 1 tenth + 3 hundredths

53. _____

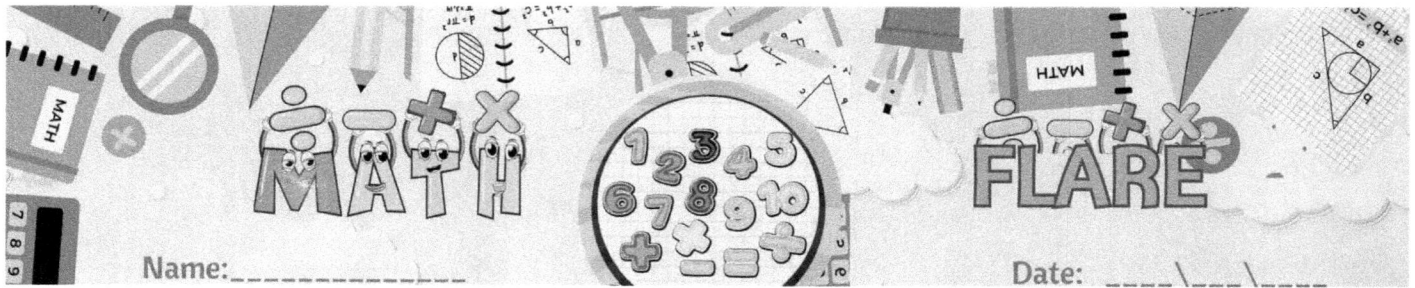

6 ten thousands + 1 thousand + 4 hundreds + 4 tens + 3 ones + 4 hundredths

54. _____

7 ten thousands + 6 hundreds + 5 tens + 4 ones + 7 tenths + 2 hundredths

55. _____

4 ten thousands + 5 thousands + 9 hundreds + 9 tens + 7 ones + 5 tenths + 7 hundredths

56. _____

5 ten thousands + 4 thousands + 8 hundreds + 8 ones + 2 hundredths

57. _____

4 ten thousands + 9 thousands + 9 hundreds + 4 tens + 1 tenth + 8 hundredths

58. _____

5 ten thousands + 8 tens + 1 tenth

59. _____

7 ten thousands + 5 hundreds + 6 tens + 7 ones + 8 tenths + 6 hundredths

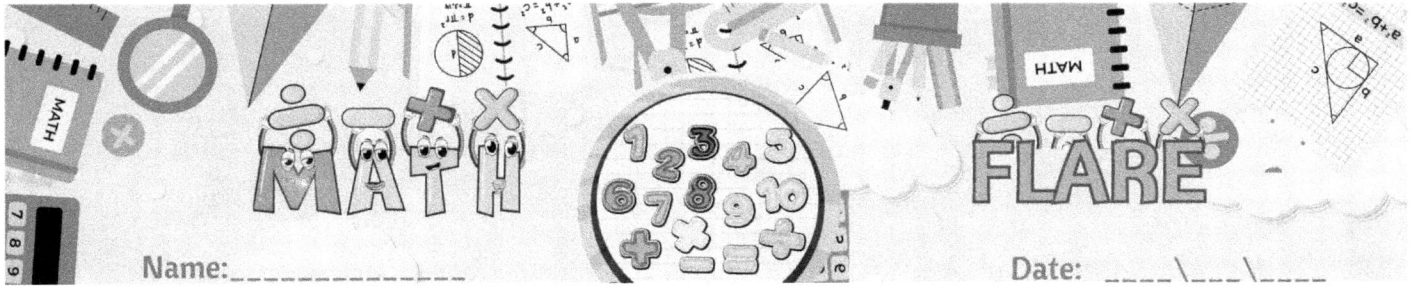

60. _____ 4 ten thousands + 4 thousands + 5 hundreds + 5 tens + 6 ones + 7 tenths + 2 hundredths

61. _____ 2 ten thousands + 9 thousands + 8 hundreds + 9 tens + 7 ones + 4 tenths + 5 hundredths

62. _____ 8 ten thousands + 1 thousand + 6 hundreds + 7 tens + 4 ones + 9 tenths + 5 hundredths

63. _____ 2 ten thousands + 4 thousands + 7 hundreds + 4 tens + 8 ones + 7 tenths + 6 hundredths

64. _____ 3 ten thousands + 3 thousands + 7 hundreds + 7 tens + 3 ones

65. _____ 3 ten thousands + 3 thousands + 4 tens + 8 tenths + 8 hundredths

66. _____ 7 ten thousands + 2 thousands + 3 hundreds + 1 ten + 8 ones + 9 tenths + 1 hundredth

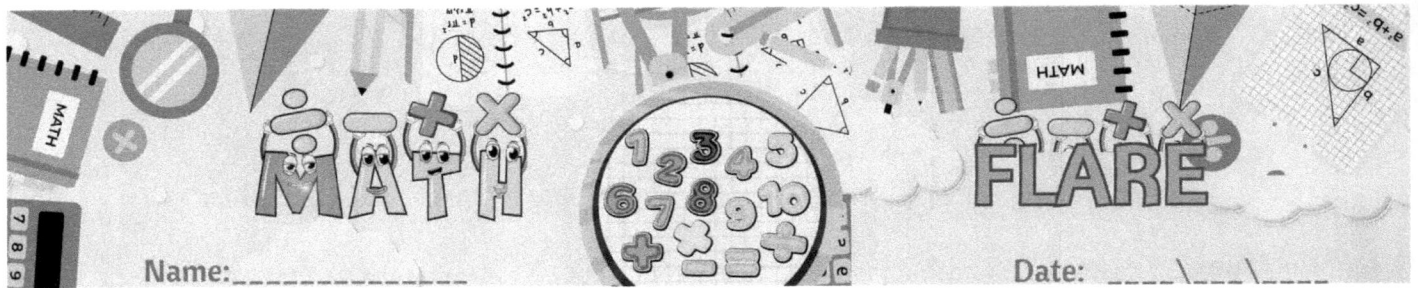

67. _____ 5 ten thousands + 7 thousands + 4 hundreds + 3 tens + 8 ones + 9 tenths + 4 hundredths

68. _____ 2 ten thousands + 1 thousand + 6 hundreds + 4 tens + 3 ones + 3 tenths + 5 hundredths

69. _____ 2 ten thousands + 9 thousands + 6 hundreds + 8 tens + 5 ones + 1 hundredth

70. _____ 9 ten thousands + 6 thousands + 1 hundred + 3 tens + 5 ones + 2 tenths + 4 hundredths

71. _____ 2 ten thousands + 6 thousands + 8 hundreds + 3 tens + 9 ones + 5 tenths + 8 hundredths

72. _____ 5 ten thousands + 2 thousands + 7 hundreds + 1 one + 9 tenths + 2 hundredths

73. _____ 1 ten thousand + 2 thousands + 4 hundreds + 8 tens + 3 ones + 7 tenths + 9 hundredths

Place Value: Expanded Notation

Provide the expanded notation for each value.

74. 882,152.64 _____

75. 705,057.42 _____

76. 693,468.01 _____

77. 756,534.26 _____

78. 424,663.82 _____
_____
_____

79. 187,751.91 _____
_____
_____

80. 353,655.79 _____
_____
_____

81. 830,758.53 _____
_____
_____

82. 853,793.26 _____
_____
_____

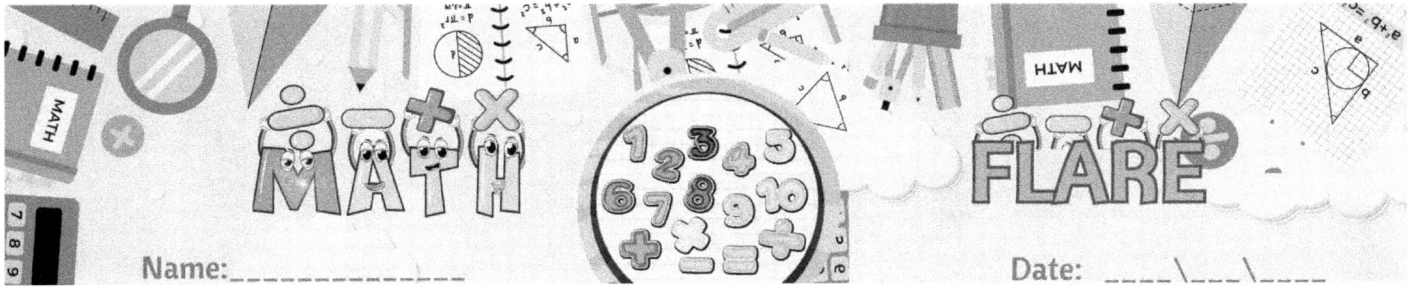

83. 270,263.23 _____
   _____
   _____

84. 449,148.63 _____
   _____
   _____

85. 230,538.72 _____
   _____
   _____

86. 349,385.51 _____
   _____
   _____

87. 367,056.16 _____
   _____
   _____

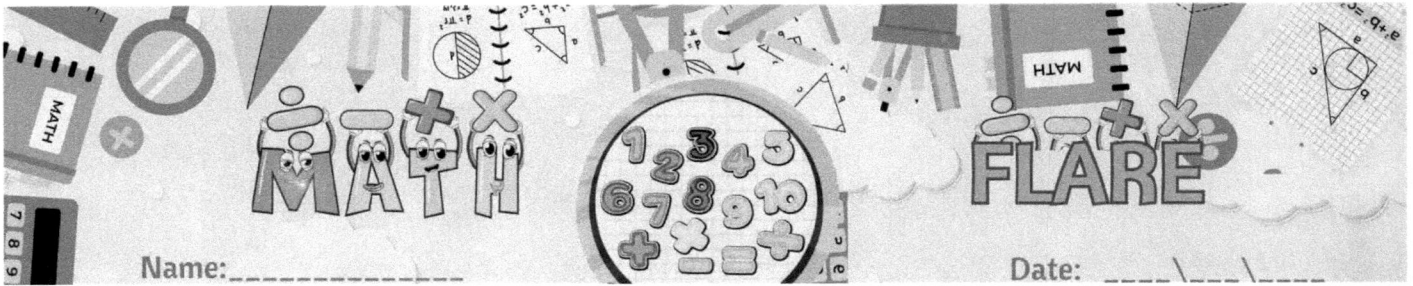

88. 415,841.43 _____
     _____
     _____

89. 194,195.81 _____
     _____
     _____

90. 758,505.42 _____
     _____
     _____

91. 237,214.90 _____
     _____
     _____

92. 278,561.12 _____
     _____
     _____

93. 488,696.73 _____
_____
_____

94. 591,225.05 _____
_____
_____

95. 126,991.96 _____
_____
_____

96. 360,068.23 _____
_____
_____

97. 761,437.00 _____
_____
_____

98. 149,333.23 _____

_____

_____

99. 482,396.24 _____

_____

_____

100. 617,647.97 _____

_____

_____

101. 976,319.80 _____

_____

_____

102. 965,012.11 _____

_____

_____

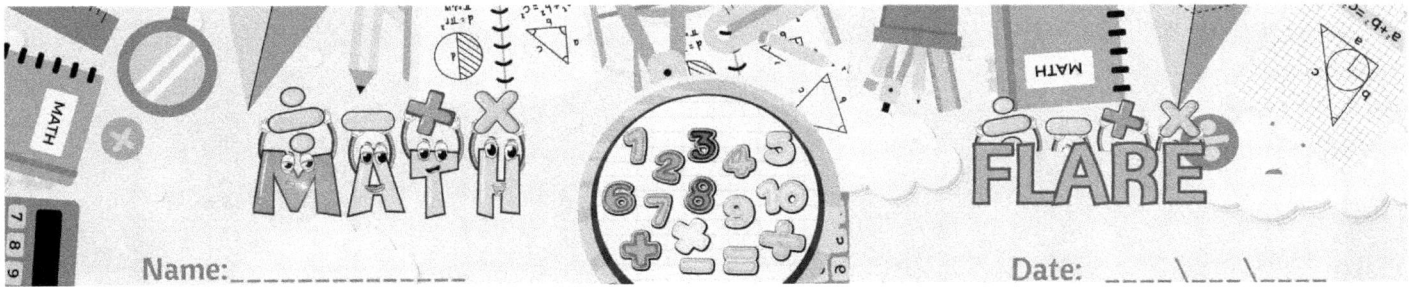

103. 511,440.66 _____
     _____
     _____

104. 983,505.30 _____
     _____
     _____

105. 591,373.69 _____
     _____
     _____

106. 155,111.62 _____
     _____
     _____

107. 502,373.44 _____
     _____
     _____

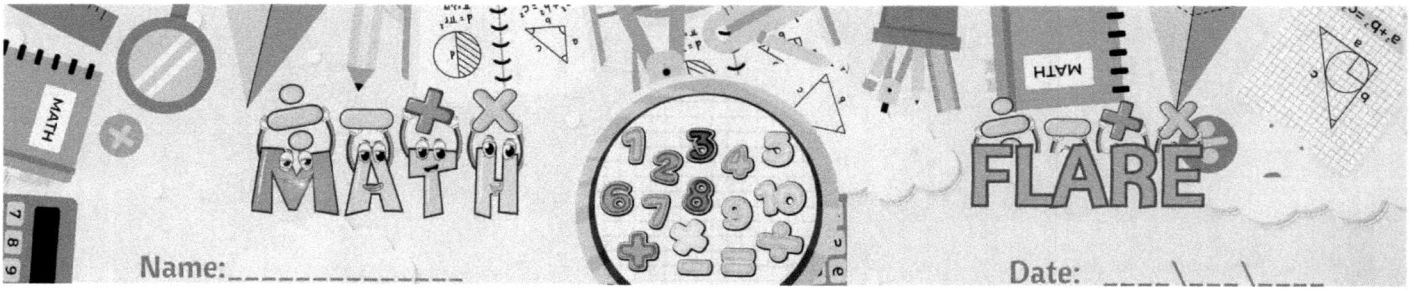

108. 732,277.84 _____
_____
_____

109. 101,489.88 _____
_____
_____

110. 766,507.71 _____
_____
_____

111. 791,545.95 _____
_____
_____

112. 174,738.02 _____
_____
_____

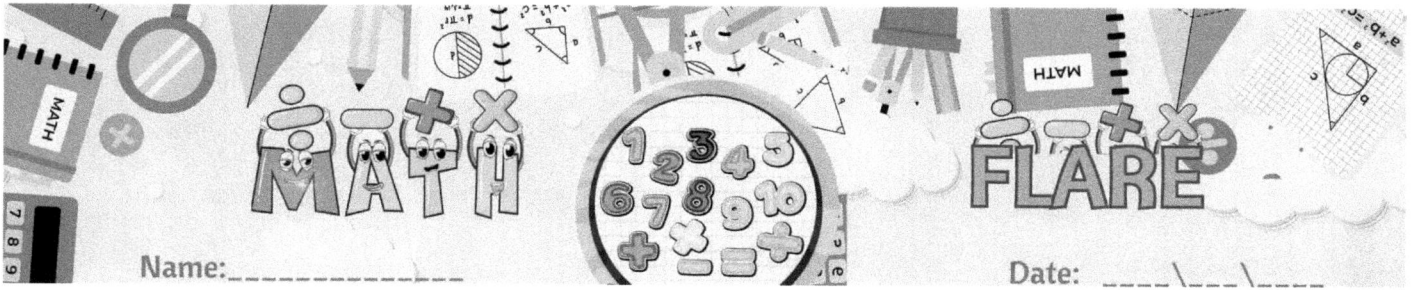

Place Value: Expanded Notation

Provide the expanded notation for each value.

113. _____ 400,000 + 10,000 + 3,000 + 40 + 9
+ 0.1 + 0.06

114. _____ 400,000 + 50,000 + 2,000 + 20 + 2
+ 0.9 + 0.02

115. _____ 600,000 + 10,000 + 4,000 + 800 + 8
+ 0.6 + 0.07

116. _____ 400,000 + 40,000 + 5,000 + 100 +
80 + 1 + 0.2 + 0.06

117. _____ 600,000 + 40,000 + 6,000 + 400 +
80 + 6 + 0.3 + 0.05

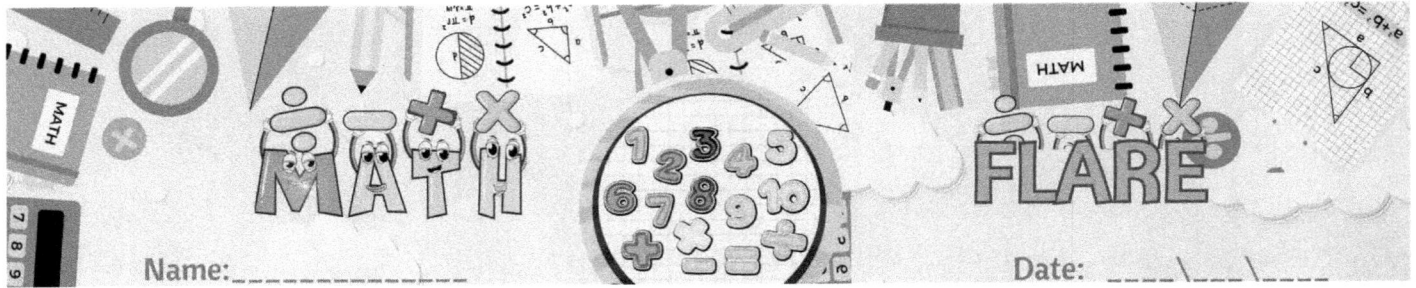

118. _____   700,000 + 90,000 + 8,000 + 300 + 30 + 9 + 0.02

119. _____   200,000 + 7,000 + 100 + 90 + 1 + 0.3 + 0.02

120. _____   900,000 + 80,000 + 1,000 + 20 + 3 + 0.2 + 0.06

121. _____   400,000 + 50,000 + 6,000 + 100 + 30 + 2 + 0.9 + 0.06

122. _____   200,000 + 50,000 + 8,000 + 500 + 40 + 8 + 0.05

123. _____   100,000 + 20,000 + 2,000 + 200 + 30 + 7 + 0.7 + 0.01

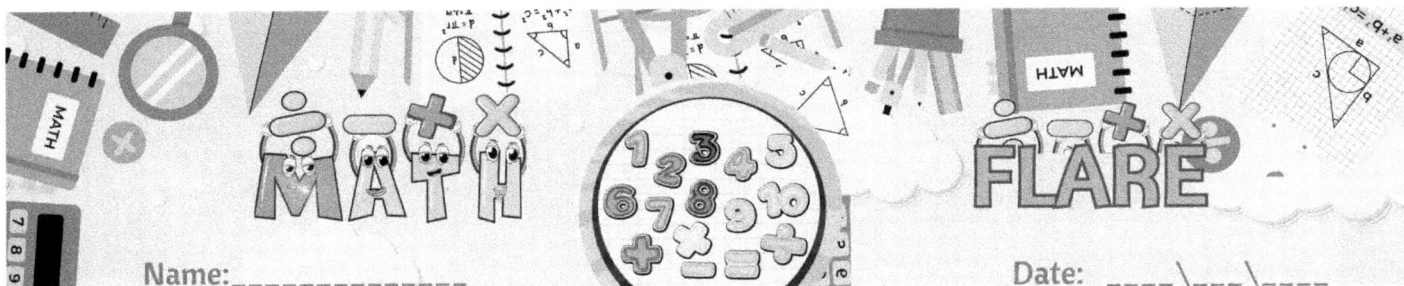

124. _____ $500{,}000 + 30{,}000 + 8{,}000 + 300 + 40 + 4 + 0.6 + 0.06$

125. _____ $800{,}000 + 20{,}000 + 4{,}000 + 100 + 30 + 7 + 0.5 + 0.07$

126. _____ $900{,}000 + 80{,}000 + 9{,}000 + 800 + 30 + 4 + 0.7$

127. _____ $100{,}000 + 30{,}000 + 8{,}000 + 300 + 20 + 2 + 0.5 + 0.01$

128. _____ $500{,}000 + 30{,}000 + 3{,}000 + 600 + 10 + 2 + 0.8 + 0.08$

129. _____ $800{,}000 + 50{,}000 + 5{,}000 + 100 + 60 + 0.6 + 0.08$

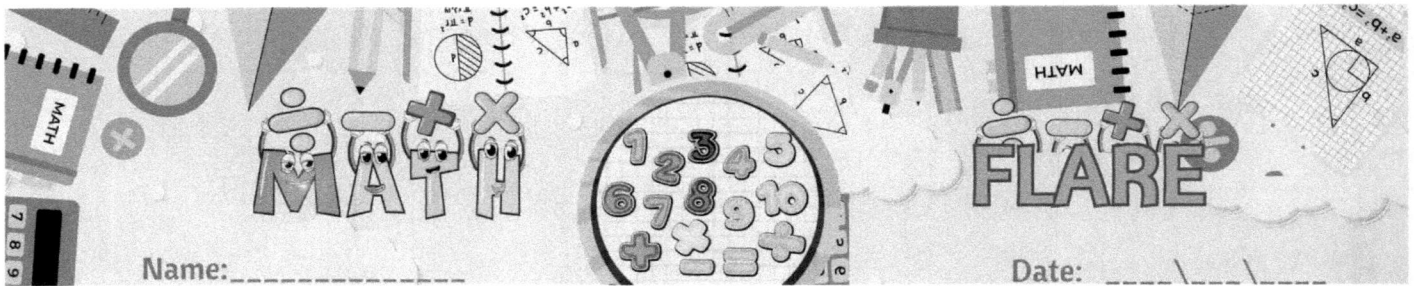

130. _____ $400{,}000 + 40{,}000 + 4{,}000 + 900 + 80 + 9 + 0.1 + 0.09$

131. _____ $900{,}000 + 30{,}000 + 2{,}000 + 30 + 1$

132. _____ $700{,}000 + 7{,}000 + 200 + 1 + 0.02$

133. _____ $900{,}000 + 40{,}000 + 2{,}000 + 200 + 60 + 7 + 0.5 + 0.08$

134. _____ $500{,}000 + 70{,}000 + 100 + 3 + 0.9 + 0.03$

135. _____ $300{,}000 + 70{,}000 + 7{,}000 + 300 + 30 + 5 + 0.9 + 0.08$

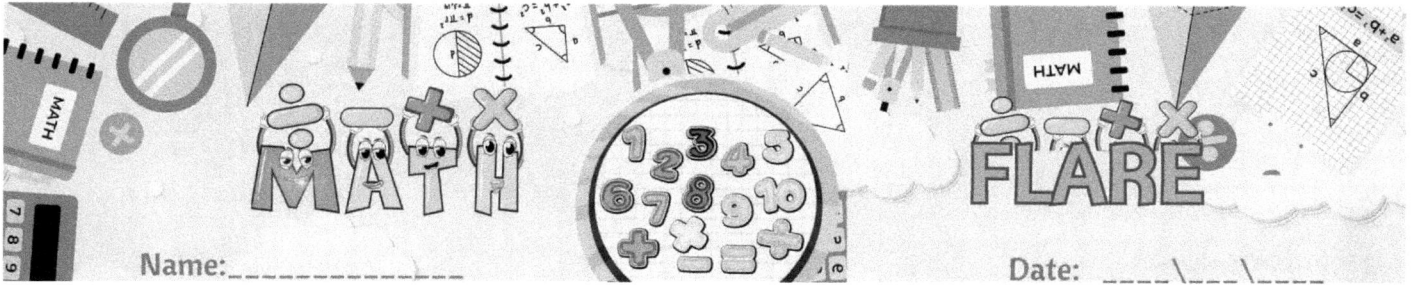

136. _____ 800,000 + 60,000 + 5,000 + 700 + 40 + 6 + 0.4 + 0.01

137. _____ 400,000 + 40,000 + 2,000 + 300 + 50 + 2 + 0.6

138. _____ 200,000 + 80,000 + 6,000 + 700 + 50 + 7 + 0.9 + 0.01

139. _____ 800,000 + 50,000 + 7,000 + 700 + 70 + 4 + 0.9 + 0.03

140. _____ 100,000 + 70,000 + 5,000 + 400 + 20 + 7 + 0.1

141. _____ 800,000 + 40,000 + 7,000 + 10 + 2 + 0.06

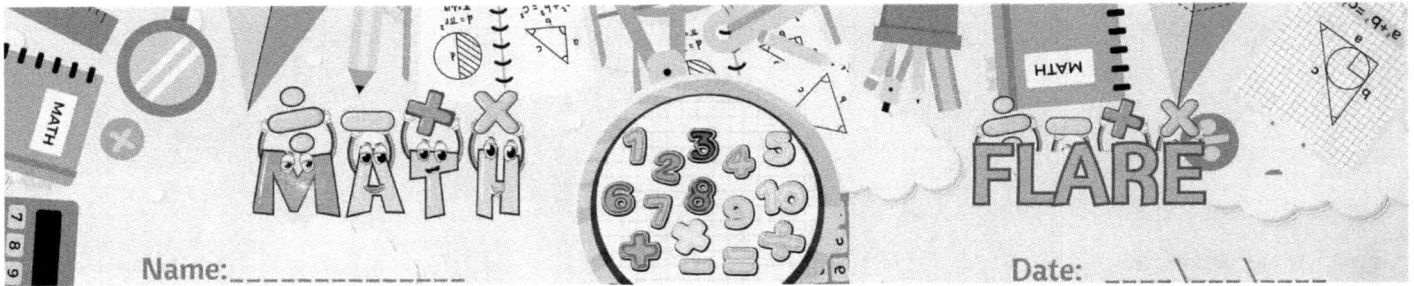

142. _____   600,000 + 30,000 + 4,000 + 700 + 70 + 8 + 0.3 + 0.02

143. _____   400,000 + 10,000 + 4,000 + 300 + 50 + 1 + 0.5 + 0.06

144. _____   400,000 + 20,000 + 7,000 + 600 + 80 + 8 + 0.09

145. _____   900,000 + 60,000 + 6,000 + 900 + 50 + 9 + 0.4 + 0.05

146. _____   100,000 + 60,000 + 2,000 + 400 + 70 + 6 + 0.8 + 0.07

147. _____   800,000 + 60,000 + 5,000 + 500 + 10 + 1 + 0.9 + 0.05

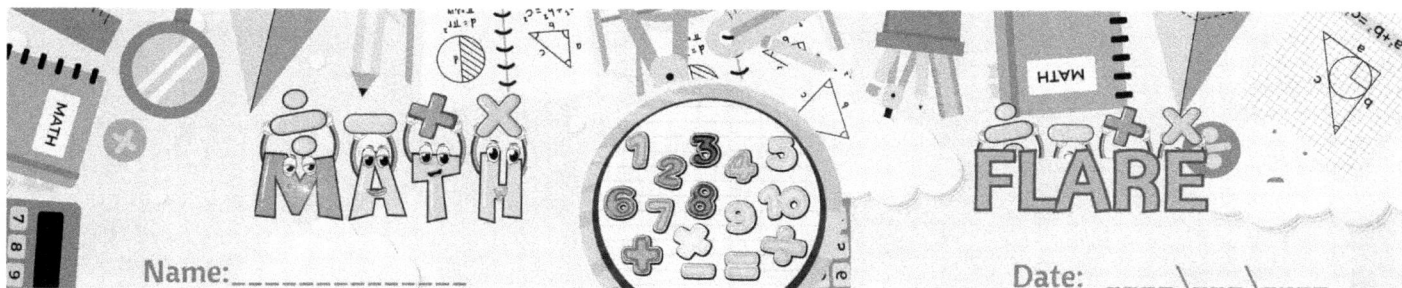

148. _____   100,000 + 30,000 + 6,000 + 600 +
                                  70 + 3 + 0.8 + 0.01

149. _____   900,000 + 70,000 + 6,000 + 400 +
                                  10 + 6 + 0.3 + 0.07

150. _____   600,000 + 80,000 + 1,000 + 800 +
                                  10 + 0.6 + 0.08

151. _____   700,000 + 10,000 + 3,000 + 500 +
                                  80 + 1 + 0.8 + 0.08

152. _____   900,000 + 60,000 + 3,000 + 90 + 7
                                  + 0.9 + 0.07

153. _____   900,000 + 40,000 + 2,000 + 100 +
                                  40 + 1 + 0.9

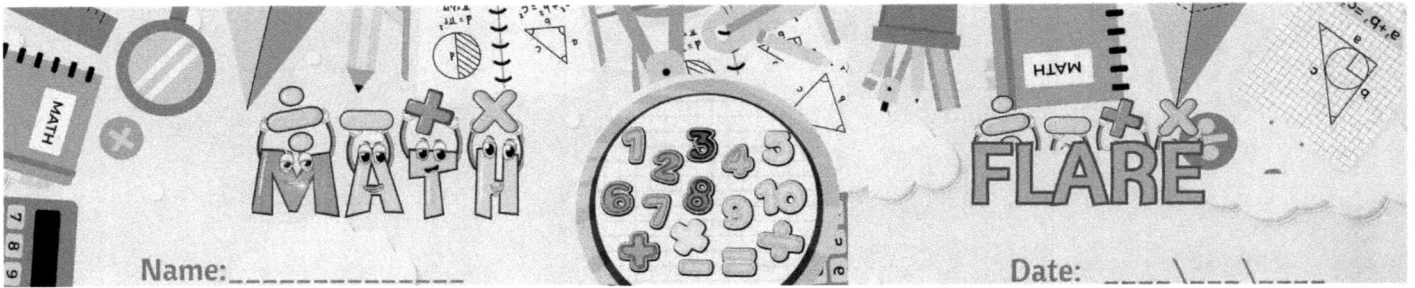

154. _____ $500,000 + 1,000 + 300 + 70 + 2 + 0.9 + 0.07$

155. _____ $200,000 + 60,000 + 1,000 + 500 + 10 + 5 + 0.01$

156. _____ $800,000 + 10,000 + 7,000 + 700 + 70 + 1 + 0.7 + 0.05$

157. _____ $900,000 + 40,000 + 2,000 + 700 + 70 + 4 + 0.4$

158. _____ $900,000 + 70,000 + 3,000 + 90 + 5 + 0.9 + 0.09$

159. _____ $200,000 + 50,000 + 9,000 + 300 + 60 + 7 + 0.7 + 0.04$

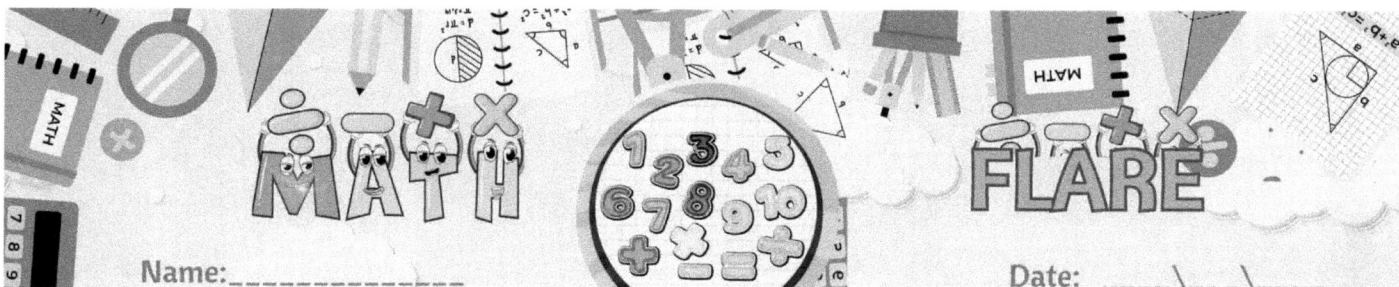

Name:_____ Date: _____

160. _____ 600,000 + 1,000 + 500 + 30 + 8 + 0.9 + 0.08

161. _____ 100,000 + 10,000 + 6,000 + 700 + 80 + 9 + 0.1

162. _____ 900,000 + 60,000 + 8,000 + 700 + 60 + 0.5 + 0.05

163. _____ 800,000 + 70,000 + 7,000 + 100 + 10 + 7 + 0.1 + 0.05

164. _____ 600,000 + 50,000 + 6,000 + 500 + 0.6 + 0.08

165. _____ 800,000 + 30,000 + 4,000 + 400 + 70 + 6 + 0.7

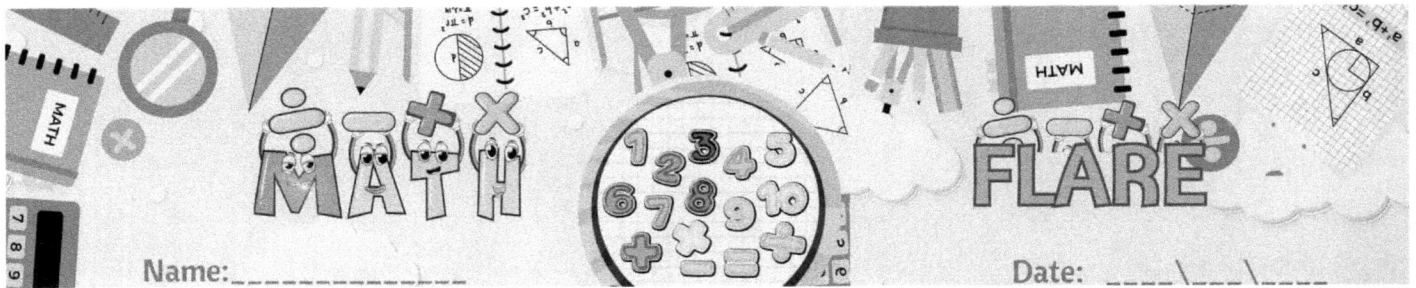

Place Value: Expanded Notation

Provide the expanded notation for each value.

166. 184,344.93 _____

167. 232,470.44 _____

168. 842,945.22 _____

169. 174,686.93 _____

170. 749,062.25 _____

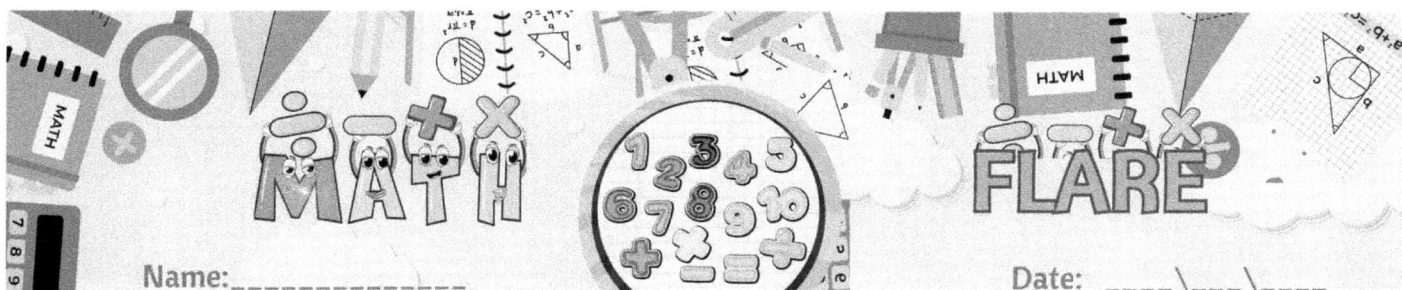

Name:_____   Date: _____

171. 102,828.67   _____
_____

172. 459,728.43   _____
_____

173. 940,564.08   _____
_____

174. 131,764.22   _____
_____

175. 234,011.20   _____
_____

176. 821,354.63   _____
_____

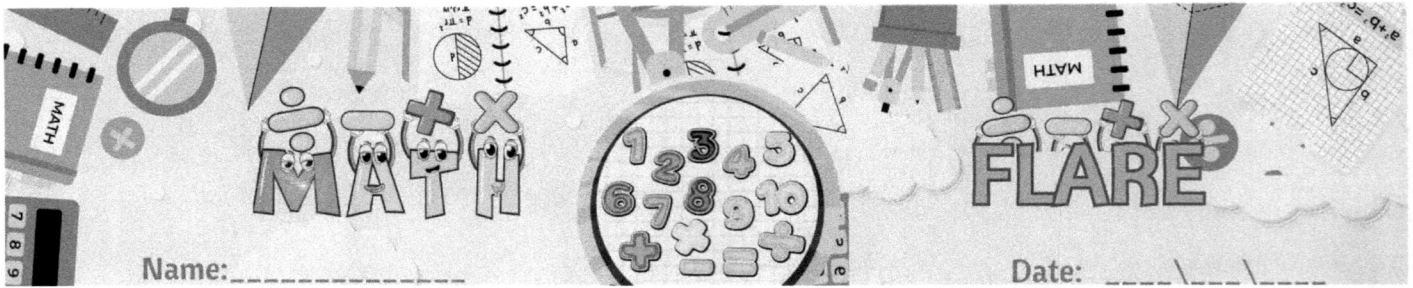

177. 844,196.49 _____

_____

178. 694,549.61 _____

_____

179. 571,385.20 _____

_____

180. 761,660.70 _____

_____

181. 224,322.75 _____

_____

182. 101,648.70 _____

_____

Name:_____

Date: _____

183. 557,196.49 _____
_____

184. 273,350.00 _____
_____

185. 731,407.30 _____
_____

186. 968,933.02 _____
_____

187. 765,059.11 _____
_____

188. 540,894.61 _____
_____

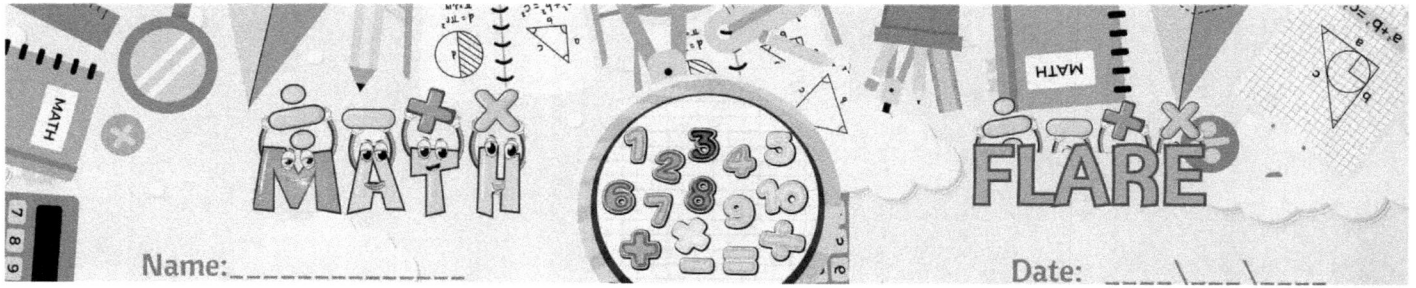

189. 408,588.92 _____
_____

190. 559,564.22 _____
_____

191. 922,972.00 _____
_____

192. 469,256.59 _____
_____

193. 127,390.18 _____
_____

194. 356,235.95 _____
_____

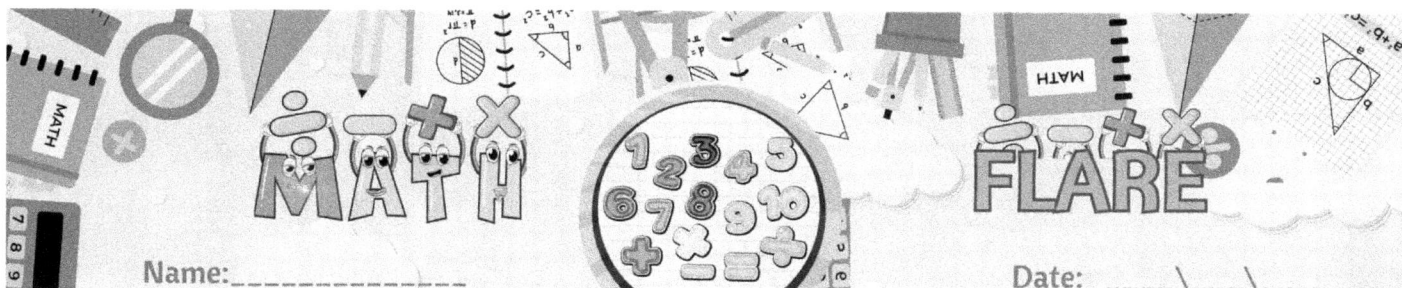

Place Value: Expanded Notation

Provide the expanded notation for each value.

195. _____ one hundred fifty-eight thousand six hundred thirty-eight

196. _____ eight hundred seventy-eight thousand two hundred fifty-one and forty-nine hundredths

197. _____ seven hundred fifty-seven thousand six hundred sixty-one and sixteen hundredths

198. _____ seven hundred fifty-seven thousand eight hundred fifty and eighty-six hundredths

199. _____ five hundred ninety-three thousand two hundred eleven and thirty-eight hundredths

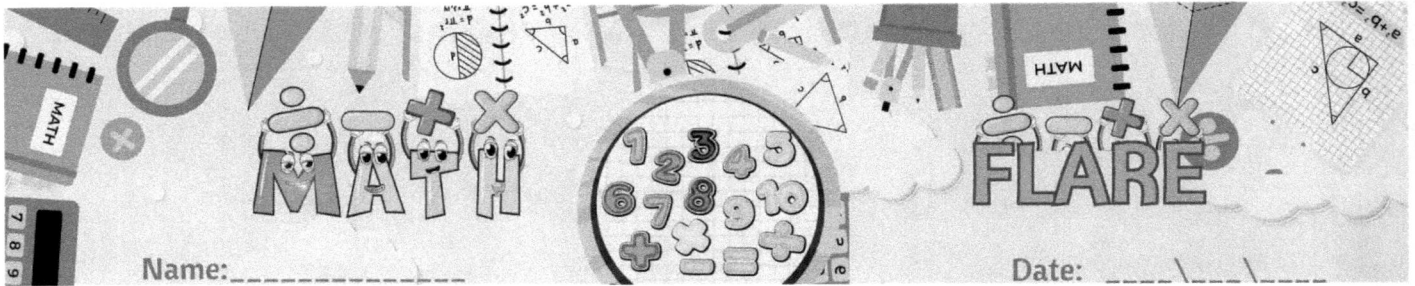

200. _____ eight hundred eighty-two thousand six hundred fourteen and fifty-three hundredths

201. _____ nine hundred thirty thousand six and forty-three hundredths

202. _____ one hundred twenty-two thousand five hundred sixty-six and seventy-three hundredths

203. _____ nine hundred sixty-one thousand nine hundred eighty-six and eighty-seven hundredths

204. _____ three hundred twenty-seven thousand three hundred fifty-four and thirteen hundredths

205. _____ six hundred seventy-eight thousand nine hundred eighty-two and one hundredth

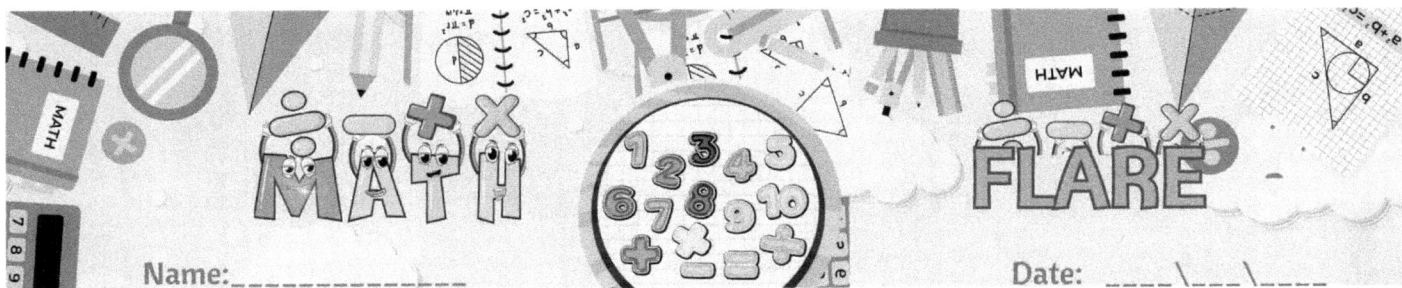

206. _____   three hundred fifty-three thousand eight hundred fifty-three and forty-four hundredths

207. _____   one hundred twenty-two thousand five hundred thirty-three and ninety hundredths

208. _____   nine hundred ten thousand three hundred seventy-seven and sixty-nine hundredths

209. _____   three hundred sixty-seven thousand three hundred sixty-one and seventy-seven hundredths

210. _____   four hundred forty thousand one hundred sixty and thirty-six hundredths

211. _____   nine hundred seventy-three thousand five hundred seventy-five and twenty-five hundredths

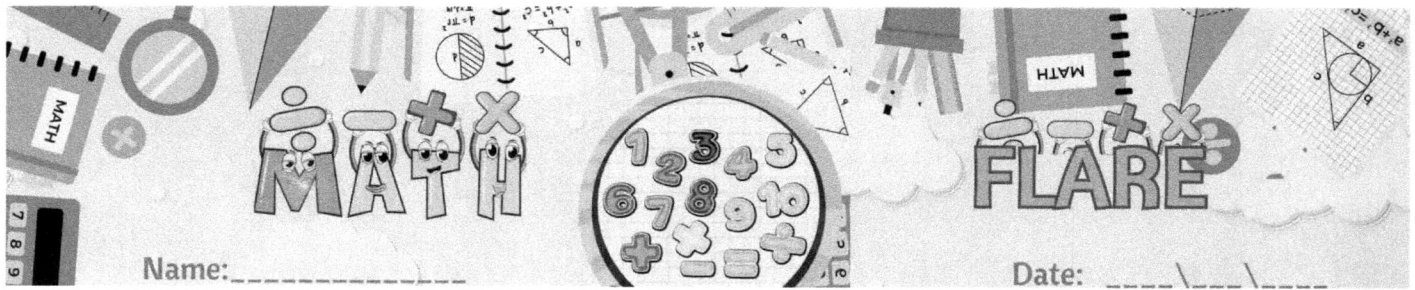

212. _____ three hundred forty-eight thousand two hundred twenty-four and seventy-nine hundredths

213. _____ five hundred one thousand seven hundred ten and seventy-nine hundredths

214. _____ four hundred ninety-seven thousand seven hundred seven and three hundredths

215. _____ four hundred seventy-seven thousand two hundred sixteen and twenty-four hundredths

216. _____ one hundred fifteen thousand one hundred forty and forty hundredths

217. _____ five hundred eleven thousand five hundred sixty-four and six hundredths

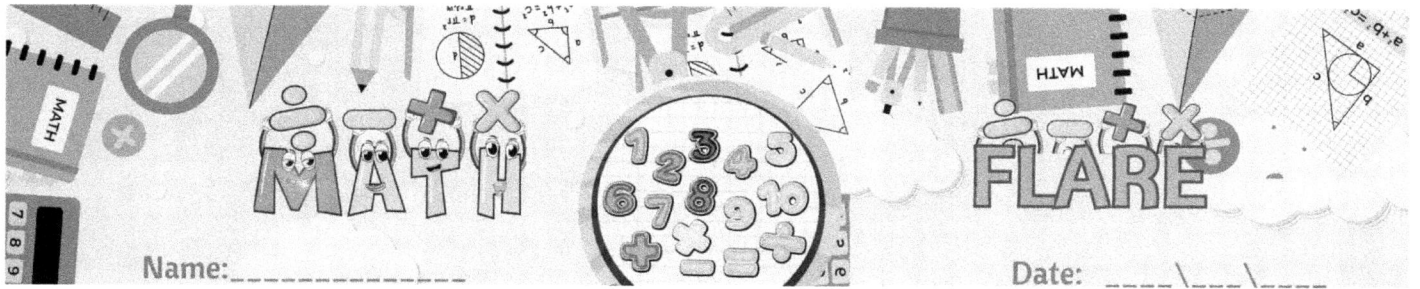

218. _____ seven hundred three thousand seven hundred sixty-seven and fifteen hundredths

219. _____ nine hundred twenty-five thousand ninety-three and thirty-seven hundredths

220. _____ eight hundred sixty-five thousand five hundred forty-three and sixty-seven hundredths

221. _____ four hundred nineteen thousand two hundred eighty-five and eighty-one hundredths

222. _____ six hundred ninety-one thousand five hundred seventy-five and eighty -two hundredths

223. _____ five hundred thirty-four thousand three hundred fifty-six and thirty hundredths

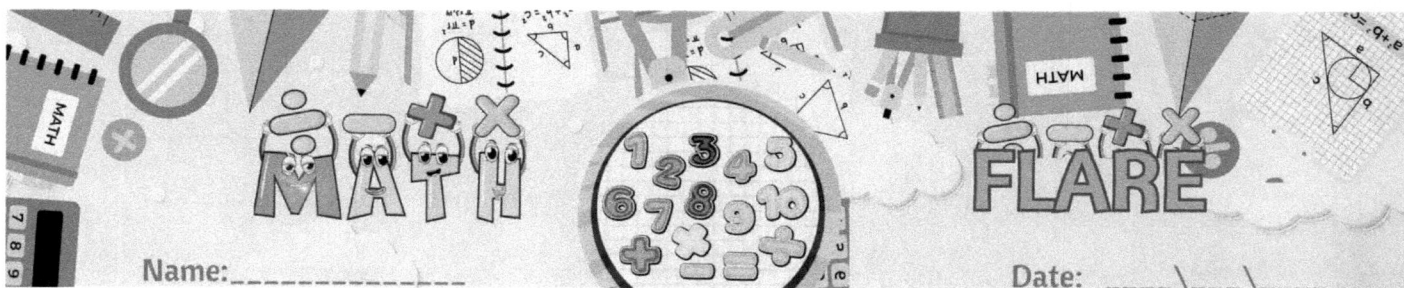

Place Value: Expanded Notation

Provide the expanded notation for each value.

224. 615,122.70 _____
_____

225. 826,090.23 _____
_____

226. 633,572.06 _____
_____

227. 432,338.25 _____
_____

228. 684,328.13 _____
_____

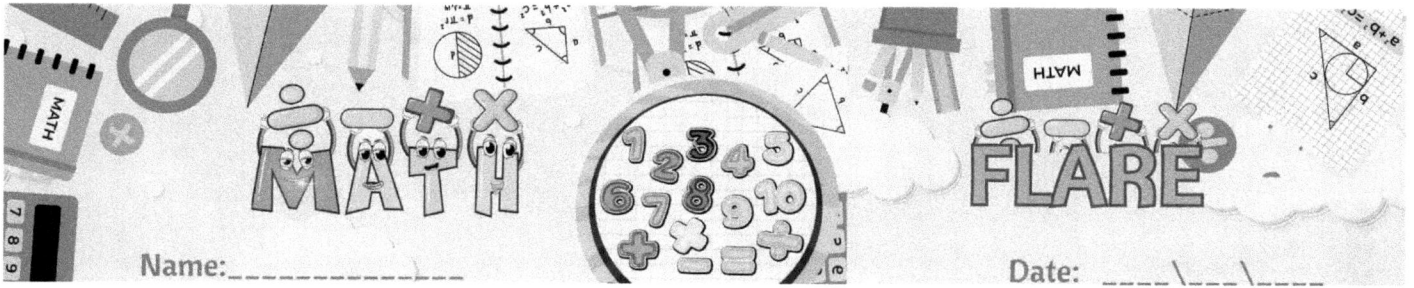

229. 973,126.21 _____

_____

230. 355,759.70 _____

_____

231. 163,693.47 _____

_____

232. 186,345.62 _____

_____

233. 201,338.23 _____

_____

234. 688,770.66 _____

_____

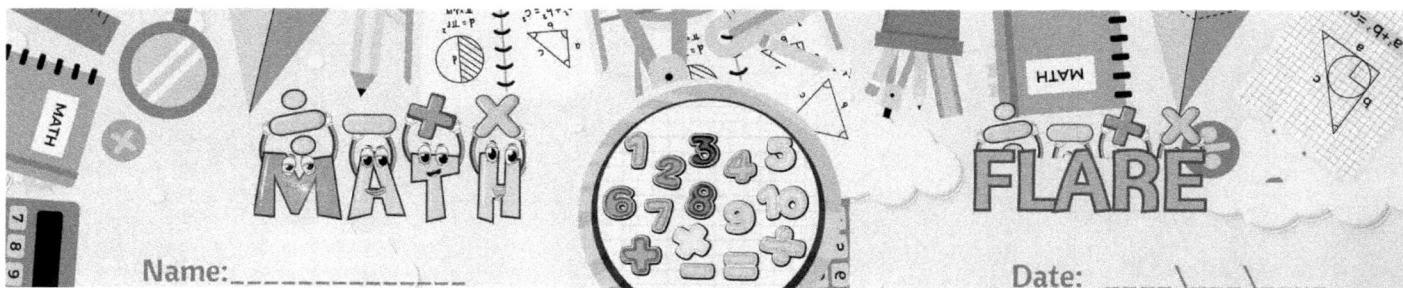

235. 831,654.26 _____
     _____

236. 201,756.02 _____
     _____

237. 139,661.82 _____
     _____

238. 329,842.37 _____
     _____

239. 594,367.97 _____
     _____

240. 477,553.86 _____
     _____

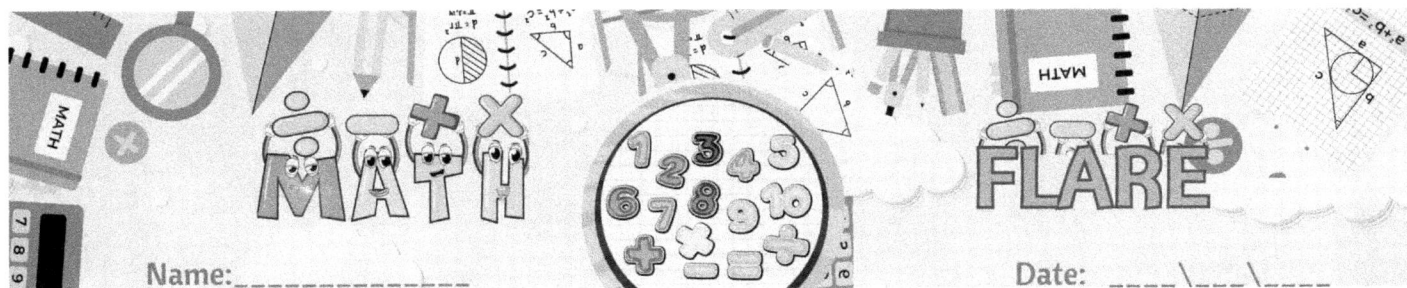

241. 946,399.12 _____

_____

242. 854,681.41 _____

_____

243. 273,532.84 _____

_____

244. 968,428.54 _____

_____

245. 585,988.96 _____

_____

246. 674,747.21 _____

_____

247. 967,545.79 _____

248. 629,683.14 _____

249. 879,019.70 _____

250. 143,497.60 _____

251. 466,687.44 _____

252. 153,894.01 _____

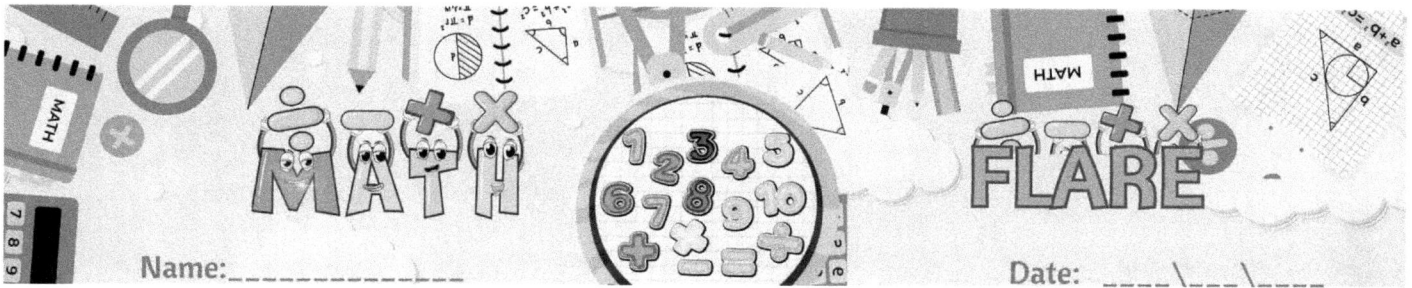

Name:_____   Date: _____

253. 832,757.48   _____

_____

254. 727,667.70   _____

_____

255. 563,328.72   _____

_____

256. 338,430.61   _____

_____

257. 588,210.41   _____

_____

258. 446,864.16   _____

_____

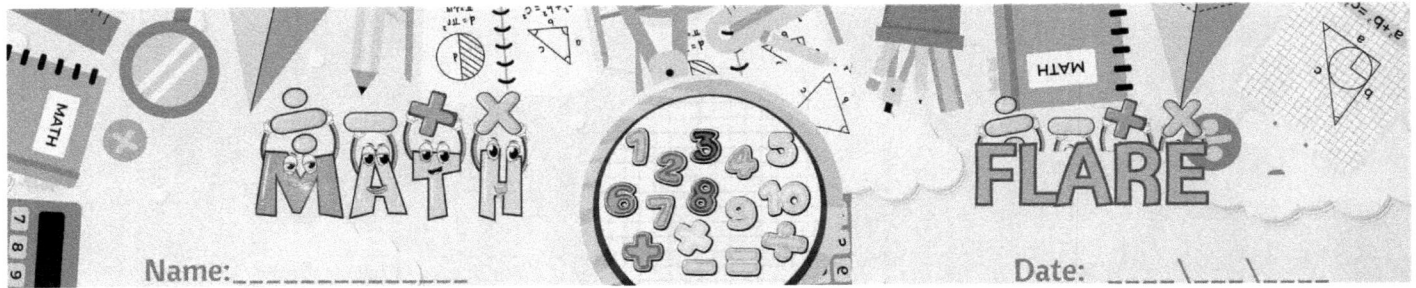

Rounding Numbers
Round to the underlined digit.

259. 5,012,638.8_4_ = _____

260. _1_,454,099.51 = _____

261. 9,2_1_5,151.88 = _____

262. 4,382,0_5_7.61 = _____

263. _9_,372,514.78 = _____

264. 1,116,02_0_.72 = _____

265. 3,764,668._9_4 = _____

266. 8,872,2_9_6.39 = _____

267. 2,_4_68,865.64 = _____

268. 8,129,_4_01.29 = _____

269. 6,660,52_7_.67 = _____

270. 3,7_5_4,602.17 = _____

271. 9,754,785.7_7_ = _____

272. 2,817,_2_16.91 = _____

273. 2,093,991.81 = _____

274. 5,475,395.21 = _____

275. 9,191,445.55 = _____

276. 5,646,043.89 = _____

277. 5,180,429.85 = _____

278. 5,659,277.54 = _____

279. 1,291,337.44 = _____

280. 2,513,430.23 = _____

281. 6,660,262.70 = _____

282. 8,026,551.15 = _____

283. 8,053,084.27 = _____

284. 9,296,286.21 = _____

285. 8,890,722.57 = _____

286. 1,097,994.64 = _____

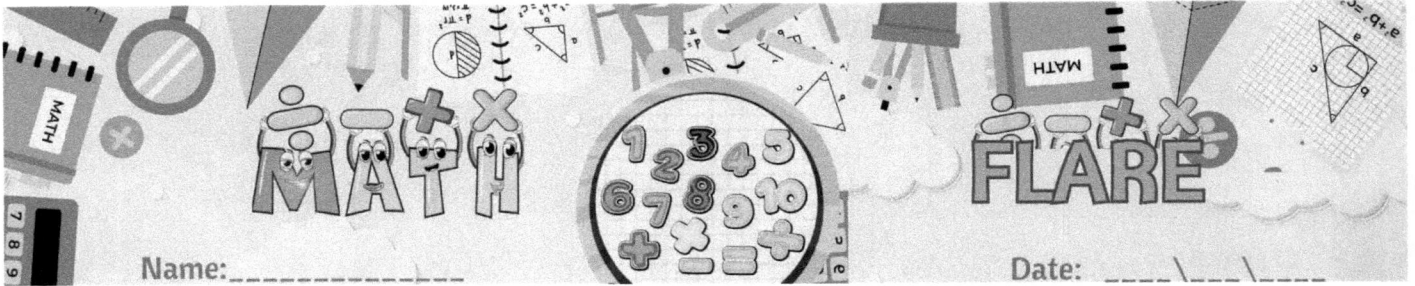

287. 3,535,881.35 = _____

288. 4,736,705.24 = _____

289. 2,254,419.44 = _____

290. 5,932,236.59 = _____

291. 6,135,456.04 = _____

292. 6,927,976.56 = _____

293. 8,285,784.86 = _____

294. 5,489,580.25 = _____

295. 5,560,386.71 = _____

296. 6,081,933.66 = _____

297. 9,174,299.40 = _____

298. 2,619,307.69 = _____

299. 6,919,616.60 = _____

300. 6,987,593.24 = _____

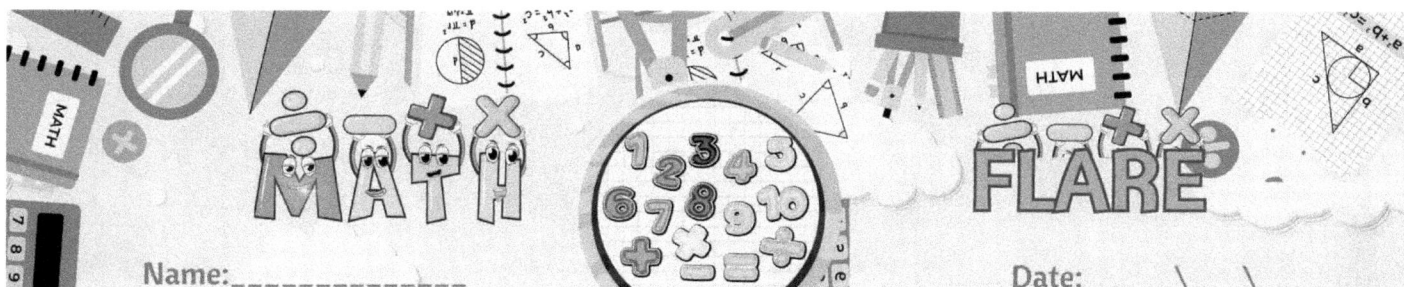

301. 5,2̲78,606.54 = _____

302. 2,546,056.6̲9 = _____

303. 9,63̲6,303.74 = _____

304. 6,035,594.9̲0 = _____

305. 1,680,19̲0.18 = _____

306. 2,849,65̲7.49 = _____

307. 9,44̲4,948.29 = _____

308. 3,852,1̲79.66 = _____

309. 8,085̲,231.48 = _____

310. 9̲,987,243.34 = _____

311. 8,203,87̲6.22 = _____

312. 1,2̲22,826.64 = _____

313. 4,177,30̲4.23 = _____

314. 3,499,2̲08.61 = _____

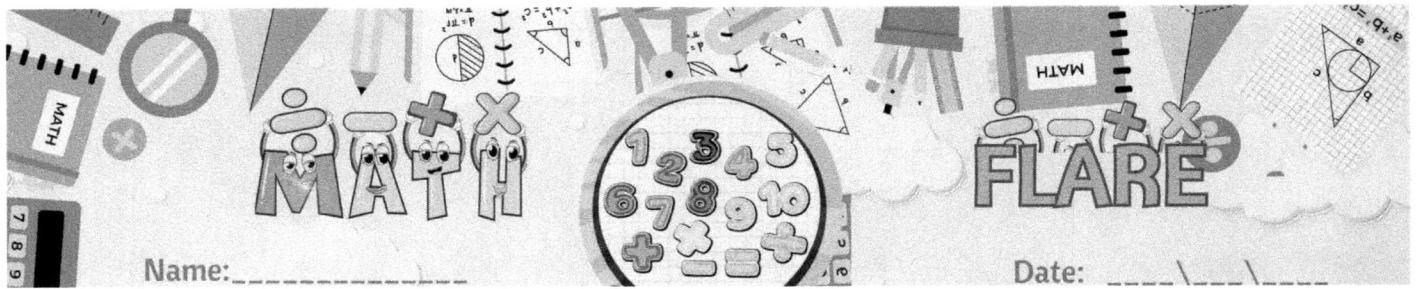

315. 4,793,836.79 = _____

316. 2,188,600.73 = _____

317. 6,328,973.33 = _____

318. 1,076,228.58 = _____

319. 2,225,298.14 = _____

320. 3,666,674.30 = _____

321. 6,336,415.03 = _____

322. 7,732,160.40 = _____

323. 6,874,981.85 = _____

324. 1,728,291.08 = _____

325. 7,619,146.12 = _____

326. 3,826,809.21 = _____

327. 4,531,432.04 = _____

328. 6,604,411.54 = _____

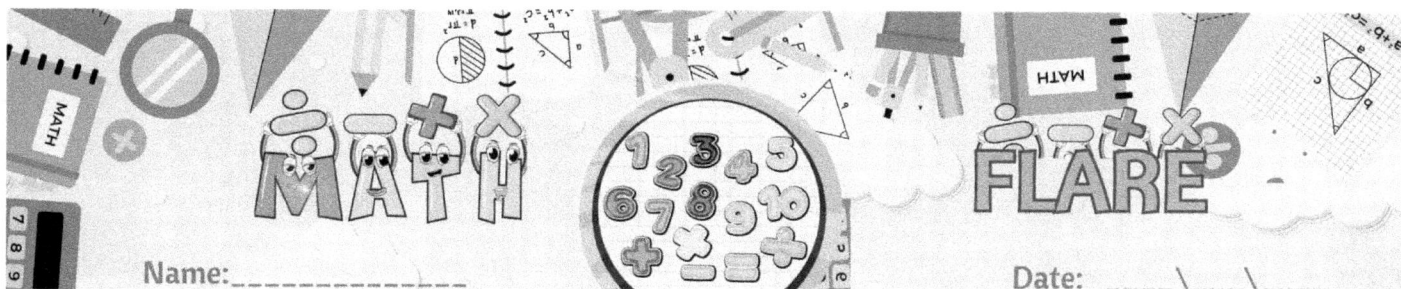

329. 9,915,008.49 = _____

330. 4,109,511.89 = _____

331. 6,471,744.47 = _____

332. 3,561,122.16 = _____

333. 8,739,660.93 = _____

334. 4,303,744.20 = _____

335. 7,234,823.68 = _____

336. 5,114,206.01 = _____

337. 8,390,247.40 = _____

338. 3,017,489.36 = _____

339. 8,616,096.02 = _____

340. 7,041,065.08 = _____

341. 1,653,046.34 = _____

342. 9,683,701.68 = _____

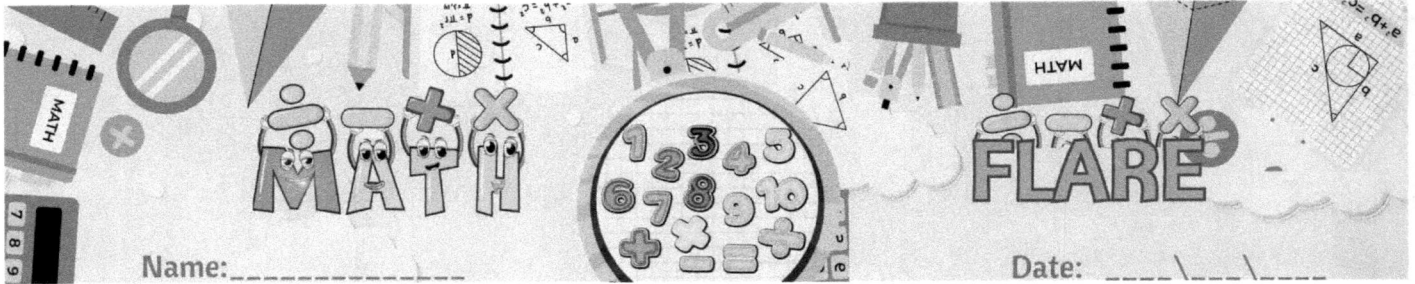

343. 6,651,4<u>7</u>3.75 = _____

344. 2,267,1<u>7</u>6.09 = _____

345. 7,728,3<u>6</u>0.36 = _____

346. <u>5</u>,912,629.40 = _____

347. <u>3</u>,750,672.33 = _____

348. 5,786,576.2<u>5</u> = _____

349. 1,6<u>9</u>5,743.46 = _____

350. 4,371,7<u>8</u>5.98 = _____

351. 9,752,<u>9</u>60.32 = _____

352. <u>9</u>,098,070.83 = _____

353. <u>1</u>,394,009.55 = _____

354. 4,252,942.<u>3</u>0 = _____

355. <u>1</u>,651,178.20 = _____

356. <u>7</u>,546,446.14 = _____

357. 5,671,074.83 = _____

358. 8,908,012.66 = _____

359. 8,416,448.77 = _____

360. 7,853,380.97 = _____

361. 8,318,225.44 = _____

362. 3,840,536.74 = _____

363. 3,937,171.16 = _____

364. 4,975,719.59 = _____

365. 4,515,498.87 = _____

366. 5,642,754.06 = _____

367. 2,483,165.70 = _____

368. 9,873,560.02 = _____

369. 6,264,384.92 = _____

370. 9,679,630.77 = _____

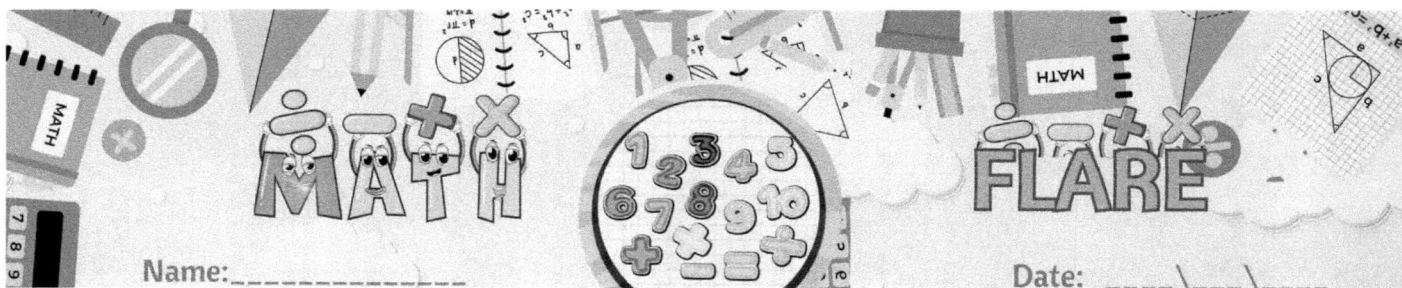

371. 3,798,353.32 = _____

372. 4,311,483.97 = _____

373. 2,460,132.54 = _____

374. 5,184,233.05 = _____

375. 3,013,627.96 = _____

376. 6,652,713.34 = _____

377. 2,080,686.65 = _____

378. 5,607,805.76 = _____

379. 3,999,930.71 = _____

380. 2,706,516.73 = _____

381. 1,076,136.88 = _____

382. 8,744,855.78 = _____

383. 5,908,668.08 = _____

384. 6,543,222.52 = _____

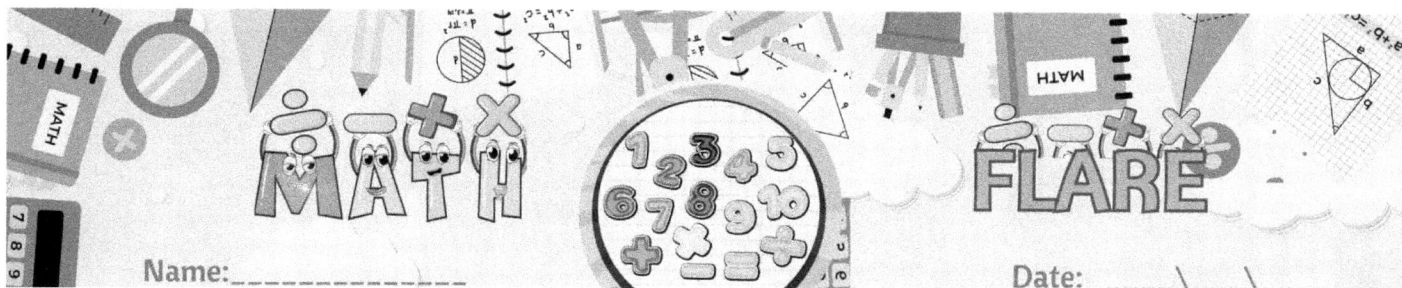

385. 4,356,551.55 = _____

386. 7,373,673.64 = _____

387. 3,167,112.61 = _____

388. 5,486,718.63 = _____

389. 3,652,566.00 = _____

390. 9,688,377.54 = _____

391. 9,443,131.17 = _____

392. 9,482,234.73 = _____

393. 4,601,040.58 = _____

394. 1,762,715.05 = _____

395. 8,722,839.64 = _____

396. 7,812,509.58 = _____

397. 6,746,530.53 = _____

398. 2,675,754.16 = _____

399. 7,751,6<u>7</u>7.21 = _____

400. 3,085,<u>6</u>06.30 = _____

401. 4,429,463.<u>6</u>9 = _____

402. 3,877,112.2<u>9</u> = _____

403. 9,522,19<u>1</u>.32 = _____

404. 2,016,1<u>1</u>2.68 = _____

405. 1,573,432.6<u>5</u> = _____

406. 6,441,4<u>7</u>6.35 = _____

407. 7,6<u>3</u>7,938.28 = _____

408. <u>6</u>,209,776.49 = _____

409. <u>2</u>,239,314.34 = _____

410. 4,99<u>8</u>,464.85 = _____

411. 6,465,<u>7</u>59.49 = _____

412. 1,063,269.0<u>7</u> = _____

ANSWERS

Page 1: Place Value

1. 1 hundredth
2. 2 millions
3. 0 hundred thousands
4. 1 ten thousand
5. 6 tens
6. 4 millions
7. 6 ones
8. 5 hundreds
9. 7 ones
10. 4 thousands
11. 1 hundredth
12. 8 hundreds
13. 7 ten thousands
14. 1 one
15. 2 hundredths
16. 6 ten thousands
17. 4 hundredths
18. 2 millions
19. 4 hundreds
20. 6 hundreds
21. 3 tens
22. 0 thousands
23. 7 hundreds
24. 0 hundreds
25. 7 hundredths
26. 5 hundreds
27. 6 millions
28. 6 millions
29. 4 thousands
30. 2 tenths
31. 3 hundreds
32. 6 tens
33. 7 tenths
34. 5 millions
35. 6 hundreds
36. 7 hundred thousands
37. 2 tens
38. 9 tens

39. 3 hundredths

Page 6: Place Value: Expanded Notation

40. 32,596.65
41. 17,681.78
42. 90,892.46
43. 38,706.32

44. 71,280.50
45. 34,083.71
46. 55,070.93
47. 18,144.56

48. 70,829.07
49. 94,485.77
50. 75,976.94
51. 58,213.08

52. 52,721.13
53. 61,443.04
54. 70,654.72
55. 45,997.57

56. 54,808.02
57. 49,940.18
58. 50,080.10
59. 70,567.86

60. 44,556.72
61. 29,897.45
62. 81,674.95
63. 24,748.76

64. 33,773.00
65. 33,040.88
66. 72,318.91
67. 57,438.94

68. 21,643.35
69. 29,685.01
70. 96,135.24
71. 26,839.58

72. 52,701.92
73. 12,483.79

Page 11: Place Value: Expanded Notation

74. 8 hundred thousands + 8 ten thousands + 2 thousands + 1 hundred + 5 tens + 2 ones + 6 tenths + 4 hundredths

75. 7 hundred thousands + 5 thousands + 5 tens + 7 ones + 4 tenths + 2 hundredths

76. 6 hundred thousands + 9 ten thousands + 3 thousands + 4 hundreds + 6 tens + 8 ones + 1 hundredth

77. 7 hundred thousands + 5 ten thousands + 6 thousands + 5 hundreds + 3 tens + 4 ones + 2 tenths + 6 hundredths

78. 4 hundred thousands + 2 ten thousands + 4 thousands + 6 hundreds + 6 tens + 3 ones + 8 tenths + 2 hundredths

79. 1 hundred thousand + 8 ten thousands + 7 thousands + 7 hundreds + 5 tens + 1 one + 9 tenths + 1 hundredth

80. 3 hundred thousands + 5 ten thousands + 3 thousands + 6 hundreds + 5 tens + 5 ones + 7 tenths + 9 hundredths

81. 8 hundred thousands + 3 ten thousands + 7 hundreds + 5 tens + 8 ones + 5 tenths + 3 hundredths

82. 8 hundred thousands + 5 ten thousands + 3 thousands + 7 hundreds + 9 tens + 3 ones + 2 tenths + 6 hundredths

83. 2 hundred thousands + 7 ten thousands + 2 hundreds + 6 tens + 3 ones + 2 tenths + 3 hundredths

84. 4 hundred thousands + 4 ten thousands + 9 thousands + 1 hundred + 4 tens + 8 ones + 6 tenths + 3 hundredths

85. 2 hundred thousands + 3 ten thousands + 5 hundreds + 3 tens + 8 ones + 7 tenths + 2 hundredths

86. 3 hundred thousands + 4 ten thousands + 9 thousands + 3 hundreds + 8 tens + 5 ones + 5 tenths + 1 hundredth

87. 3 hundred thousands + 6 ten thousands + 7 thousands + 5 tens + 6 ones + 1 tenth + 6 hundredths

88. 4 hundred thousands + 1 ten thousand + 5 thousands + 8 hundreds + 4 tens + 1 one + 4 tenths + 3 hundredths

89. 1 hundred thousand + 9 ten thousands + 4 thousands + 1 hundred + 9 tens + 5 ones + 8 tenths + 1 hundredth

90. 7 hundred thousands + 5 ten thousands + 8 thousands + 5 hundreds + 5 ones + 4 tenths + 2 hundredths

91. 2 hundred thousands + 3 ten thousands + 7 thousands + 2 hundreds + 1 ten + 4 ones + 9 tenths

92. 2 hundred thousands + 7 ten thousands + 8 thousands + 5 hundreds + 6 tens + 1 one + 1 tenth + 2 hundredths

93. 4 hundred thousands + 8 ten thousands + 8 thousands + 6 hundreds + 9 tens + 6 ones + 7 tenths + 3 hundredths

94. 5 hundred thousands + 9 ten thousands + 1 thousand + 2 hundreds + 2 tens + 5 ones + 5 hundredths

95. 1 hundred thousand + 2 ten thousands + 6 thousands + 9 hundreds + 9 tens + 1 one + 9 tenths + 6 hundredths

96. 3 hundred thousands + 6 ten thousands + 6 tens + 8 ones + 2 tenths + 3 hundredths

97. 7 hundred thousands + 6 ten thousands + 1 thousand + 4 hundreds + 3 tens + 7 ones

98. 1 hundred thousand + 4 ten thousands + 9 thousands + 3 hundreds + 3 tens + 3 ones + 2 tenths + 3 hundredths

99. 4 hundred thousands + 8 ten thousands + 2 thousands + 3 hundreds + 9 tens + 6 ones + 2 tenths + 4 hundredths

100. 6 hundred thousands + 1 ten thousand + 7 thousands + 6 hundreds + 4 tens + 7 ones + 9 tenths + 7 hundredths

101. 9 hundred thousands + 7 ten thousands + 6 thousands + 3 hundreds + 1 ten + 9 ones + 8 tenths

102. 9 hundred thousands + 6 ten thousands + 5 thousands + 1 ten + 2 ones + 1 tenth + 1 hundredth

103. 5 hundred thousands + 1 ten thousand + 1 thousand + 4 hundreds + 4 tens + 6 tenths + 6 hundredths

104. 9 hundred thousands + 8 ten thousands + 3 thousands + 5 hundreds + 5 ones + 3 tenths

105. 5 hundred thousands + 9 ten thousands + 1 thousand + 3 hundreds + 7 tens + 3 ones + 6 tenths + 9 hundredths

106. 1 hundred thousand + 5 ten thousands + 5 thousands + 1 hundred + 1 ten + 1 one + 6 tenths + 2 hundredths

107. 5 hundred thousands + 2 thousands + 3 hundreds + 7 tens + 3 ones + 4 tenths + 4 hundredths

108. 7 hundred thousands + 3 ten thousands + 2 thousands + 2 hundreds + 7 tens + 7 ones + 8 tenths + 4 hundredths

109. 1 hundred thousand + 1 thousand + 4 hundreds + 8 tens + 9 ones + 8 tenths + 8 hundredths

110. 7 hundred thousands + 6 ten thousands + 6 thousands + 5 hundreds + 7 ones + 7 tenths + 1 hundredth

111. 7 hundred thousands + 9 ten thousands + 1 thousand + 5 hundreds + 4 tens + 5 ones + 9 tenths + 5 hundredths

112. 1 hundred thousand + 7 ten thousands + 4 thousands + 7 hundreds + 3 tens + 8 ones + 2 hundredths

Page 19: Place Value: Expanded Notation

113. 413,049.16
114. 452,022.92
115. 614,808.67
116. 445,181.26
117. 646,486.35
118. 798,339.02
119. 207,191.32
120. 981,023.26
121. 456,132.96
122. 258,548.05
123. 122,237.71
124. 538,344.66
125. 824,137.57
126. 989,834.70
127. 138,322.51
128. 533,612.88

129. 855,160.68   130. 444,989.19   131. 932,031.00   132. 707,201.02

133. 942,267.58   134. 570,103.93   135. 377,335.98   136. 865,746.41

137. 442,352.60   138. 286,757.91   139. 857,774.93   140. 175,427.10

141. 847,012.06   142. 634,778.32   143. 414,351.56   144. 427,688.09

145. 966,959.45   146. 162,476.87   147. 865,511.95   148. 136,673.81

149. 976,416.37   150. 681,810.68   151. 713,581.88   152. 963,097.97

153. 942,141.90   154. 501,372.97   155. 261,515.01   156. 817,771.75

157. 942,774.40   158. 973,095.99   159. 259,367.74   160. 601,538.98

161. 116,789.10   162. 968,760.55   163. 877,117.15   164. 656,500.68

165. 834,476.70

Page 28:   Place Value: Expanded Notation

166. 100,000 + 80,000 + 4,000 + 300 + 40 + 4 + 0.9 + 0.03

167. 200,000 + 30,000 + 2,000 + 400 + 70 + 0.4 + 0.04

168. 800,000 + 40,000 + 2,000 + 900 + 40 + 5 + 0.2 + 0.02

169. 100,000 + 70,000 + 4,000 + 600 + 80 + 6 + 0.9 + 0.03

170. 700,000 + 40,000 + 9,000 + 60 + 2 + 0.2 + 0.05

171. 100,000 + 2,000 + 800 + 20 + 8 + 0.6 + 0.07

172. 400,000 + 50,000 + 9,000 + 700 + 20 + 8 + 0.4 + 0.03

173. 900,000 + 40,000 + 500 + 60 + 4 + 0.08

174. 100,000 + 30,000 + 1,000 + 700 + 60 + 4 + 0.2 + 0.02

175. 200,000 + 30,000 + 4,000 + 10 + 1 + 0.2

176. 800,000 + 20,000 + 1,000 + 300 + 50 + 4 + 0.6 + 0.03

177. 800,000 + 40,000 + 4,000 + 100 + 90 + 6 + 0.4 + 0.09

178. 600,000 + 90,000 + 4,000 + 500 + 40 + 9 + 0.6 + 0.01

179. 500,000 + 70,000 + 1,000 + 300 + 80 + 5 + 0.2

180. 700,000 + 60,000 + 1,000 + 600 + 60 + 0.7

181. 200,000 + 20,000 + 4,000 + 300 + 20 + 2 + 0.7 + 0.05

182. 100,000 + 1,000 + 600 + 40 + 8 + 0.7

183. 500,000 + 50,000 + 7,000 + 100 + 90 + 6 + 0.4 + 0.09

184. 200,000 + 70,000 + 3,000 + 300 + 50

185. 700,000 + 30,000 + 1,000 + 400 + 7 + 0.3

186. 900,000 + 60,000 + 8,000 + 900 + 30 + 3 + 0.02

187. 700,000 + 60,000 + 5,000 + 50 + 9 + 0.1 + 0.01

188. 500,000 + 40,000 + 800 + 90 + 4 + 0.6 + 0.01

189. 400,000 + 8,000 + 500 + 80 + 8 + 0.9 + 0.02

190. 500,000 + 50,000 + 9,000 + 500 + 60 + 4 + 0.2 + 0.02

191. 900,000 + 20,000 + 2,000 + 900 + 70 + 2

192. 400,000 + 60,000 + 9,000 + 200 + 50 + 6 + 0.5 + 0.09

193. 100,000 + 20,000 + 7,000 + 300 + 90 + 0.1 + 0.08

194. 300,000 + 50,000 + 6,000 + 200 + 30 + 5 + 0.9 + 0.05

Page 33: Place Value: Expanded Notation

195. 158,638.00   196. 878,251.49   197. 757,661.16

198. 757,850.86   199. 593,211.38   200. 882,614.53

201. 930,006.43   202. 122,566.73   203. 961,986.87

204. 327,354.13   205. 678,982.01   206. 353,853.44

207. 122,533.90   208. 910,377.69   209. 367,361.77

210. 440,160.36   211. 973,575.25   212. 348,224.79

213. 501,710.79   214. 497,707.03   215. 477,216.24

216. 115,140.40   217. 511,564.06   218. 703,767.15

219. 925,093.37   220. 865,543.67   221. 419,285.81

222. 691,575.82   223. 534,356.30

Page 38: Place Value: Expanded Notation

224. six hundred fifteen thousand one hundred twenty-two and seventy hundredths

225. eight hundred twenty-six thousand ninety and twenty-three hundredths

226. six hundred thirty-three thousand five hundred seventy-two and six hundredths

227. four hundred thirty-two thousand three hundred thirty-eight and twenty-five hundredths

228. six hundred eighty-four thousand three hundred twenty-eight and thirteen hundredths

229. nine hundred seventy-three thousand one hundred twenty-six and twenty-one hundredths

230. three hundred fifty-five thousand seven hundred fifty-nine and seventy hundredths

231. one hundred sixty-three thousand six hundred ninety-three and forty-seven hundredths

232. one hundred eighty-six thousand three hundred forty-five and sixty-two hundredths

233. two hundred one thousand three hundred thirty-eight and twenty-three hundredths

234. six hundred eighty-eight thousand seven hundred seventy and sixty-six hundredths

235. eight hundred thirty-one thousand six hundred fifty-four and twenty-six hundredths

236. two hundred one thousand seven hundred fifty-six and two hundredths

237. one hundred thirty-nine thousand six hundred sixty-one and eighty-two hundredths

238. three hundred twenty-nine thousand eight hundred forty-two and thirty-seven hundredths

239. five hundred ninety-four thousand three hundred sixty-seven and ninety-seven hundredths

240. four hundred seventy-seven thousand five hundred fifty-three and eighty-six hundredths

241. nine hundred forty-six thousand three hundred ninety-nine and twelve hundredths

242. eight hundred fifty-four thousand six hundred eighty-one and forty-one hundredths

243. two hundred seventy-three thousand five hundred thirty-two and eighty-four hundredths

244. nine hundred sixty-eight thousand four hundred twenty-eight and fifty-four hundredths

245. five hundred eighty-five thousand nine hundred eighty-eight and ninety-six hundredths

246. six hundred seventy-four thousand seven hundred forty-seven and twenty-one hundredths

247. nine hundred sixty-seven thousand five hundred forty-five and seventy-nine hundredths

248. six hundred twenty-nine thousand six hundred eighty-three and fourteen hundredths

249. eight hundred seventy-nine thousand nineteen and seventy hundredths

250. one hundred forty-three thousand four hundred ninety-seven and sixty hundredths

251. four hundred sixty-six thousand six hundred eighty-seven and forty-four hundredths

252. one hundred fifty-three thousand eight hundred ninety-four and one hundredth

253. eight hundred thirty-two thousand seven hundred fifty-seven and forty-eight hundredths

254. seven hundred twenty-seven thousand six hundred sixty-seven and seventy hundredths

255. five hundred sixty-three thousand three hundred twenty-eight and seventy-two hundredths

256. three hundred thirty-eight thousand four hundred thirty and sixty-one hundredths

257. five hundred eighty-eight thousand two hundred ten and forty-one hundredths

258. four hundred forty-six thousand eight hundred sixty-four and sixteen hundredths

Page 44: Rounding Numbers

259. 5,012,638.84

260. 1,000,000

261. 9,220,000

262. 4,382,060

263. 9,000,000

264. 1,116,021

265. 3,764,668.9

266. 8,872,300

267. 2,500,000

268. 8,129,400

269. 6,660,528

270. 3,750,000

271. 9,754,785.77

272. 2,817,200

273. 2,000,000

274. 5,475,395

275. 9,191,445.6

276. 5,646,040

277. 5,000,000

278. 5,659,000

279. 1,291,300

280. 2,513,000

281. 6,660,260

282. 8,026,551.15

283. 8,053,084

284. 9,296,300

285. 8,900,000

286. 1,100,000

287. 3,535,881

288. 5,000,000

289. 2,254,420

290. 5,900,000

291. 6,140,000

292. 6,927,977

293. 8,285,800

294. 5,489,580

295. 5,560,386.7

296. 6,080,000

297. 9,174,300

298. 2,619,310

299. 6,919,600

300. 6,987,593.24

301. 5,300,000

302. 2,546,056.7

303. 9,636,000

304. 6,035,594.9

305. 1,680,190

306. 2,849,660

307. 9,445,000

308. 3,852,200

309. 8,085,000

310. 10,000,000

311. 8,203,880

312. 1,200,000

313. 4,177,300

314. 3,499,200

315. 4,794,000

316. 2,190,000

317. 6,328,973.3

318. 1,076,230

319. 2,225,300

320. 3,666,670

321. 6,336,415.03

322. 7,700,000

323. 6,874,981.9

324. 1,728,300

325. 7,619,146.12

326. 3,830,000

327. 5,000,000

328. 6,604,000

329. 9,915,008.5

330. 4,109,500

331. 6,471,744.47

332. 3,561,100

333. 8,739,660.9

334. 4,303,740

335. 7,230,000

336. 5,114,206

337. 8,390,250

338. 3,017,489.36

339. 8,616,096

340. 7,041,070

341. 1,653,046.3

342. 9,700,000

343. 6,651,470

344. 2,267,180

345. 7,728,360

346. 6,000,000

347. 4,000,000

348. 5,786,576.25

349. 1,700,000

350. 4,371,790

351. 9,753,000

352. 9,000,000

353. 1,000,000

354. 4,252,942.3

355. 2,000,000

356. 8,000,000

357. 6,000,000

358. 8,908,012.7

359. 8,416,448.8

360. 7,853,400

361. 8,318,200

362. 3,840,536.74

363. 3,937,171

364. 4,975,719.6

365. 5,000,000

366. 6,000,000

367. 2,480,000

368. 10,000,000

369. 6,260,000

370. 9,679,631

371. 3,798,350

372. 4,311,484

373. 2,460,132.5

374. 5,184,233.05

375. 3,013,628

376. 6,652,713

377. 2,080,700

378. 5,600,000

379. 3,999,930.7

380. 2,706,516.7

381. 1,100,000

382. 9,000,000

383. 5,900,000

384. 6,540,000

385. 4,000,000

386. 7,373,673.64

387. 3,167,100

388. 5,000,000

389. 3,652,600

390. 9,700,000

391. 9,443,130

392. 9,482,234.7

393. 5,000,000

394. 1,760,000

395. 9,000,000

396. 7,812,509.6

397. 6,746,500

398. 2,675,754.2

399. 7,751,680

400. 3,085,600

401. 4,429,463.7

402. 3,877,112.29

403. 9,522,191

404. 2,016,100

405. 1,573,432.65

406. 6,441,480

407. 7,640,000

408. 6,000,000

409. 2,000,000

410. 4,998,000

411. 6,465,800

412. 1,063,269.07

Printed in the USA
CPSIA information can be obtained
at www.ICGtesting.com
LVHW081229240924
791983LV00012B/305